This book belongs to:

____

SPACE PUBLISHING

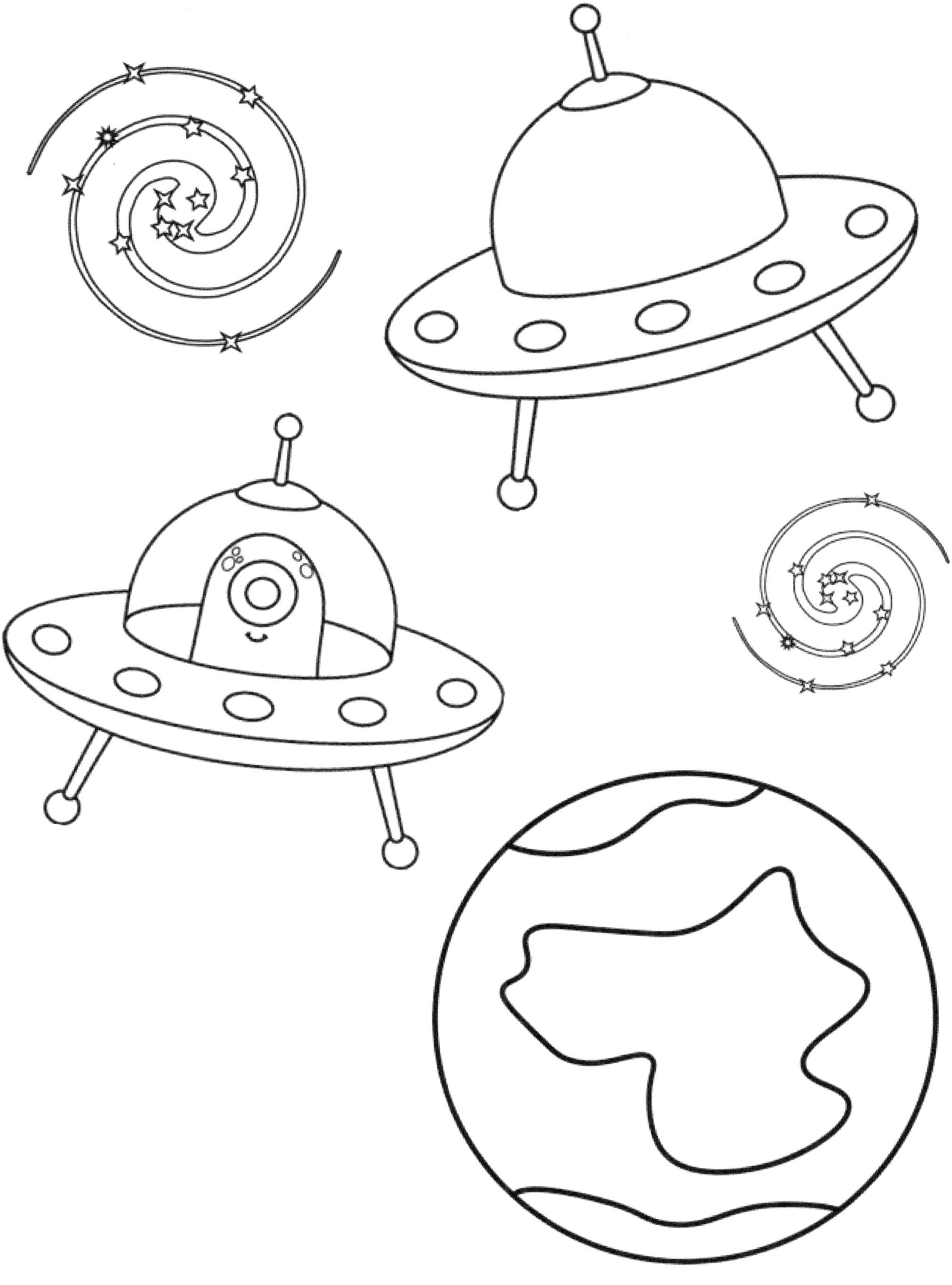

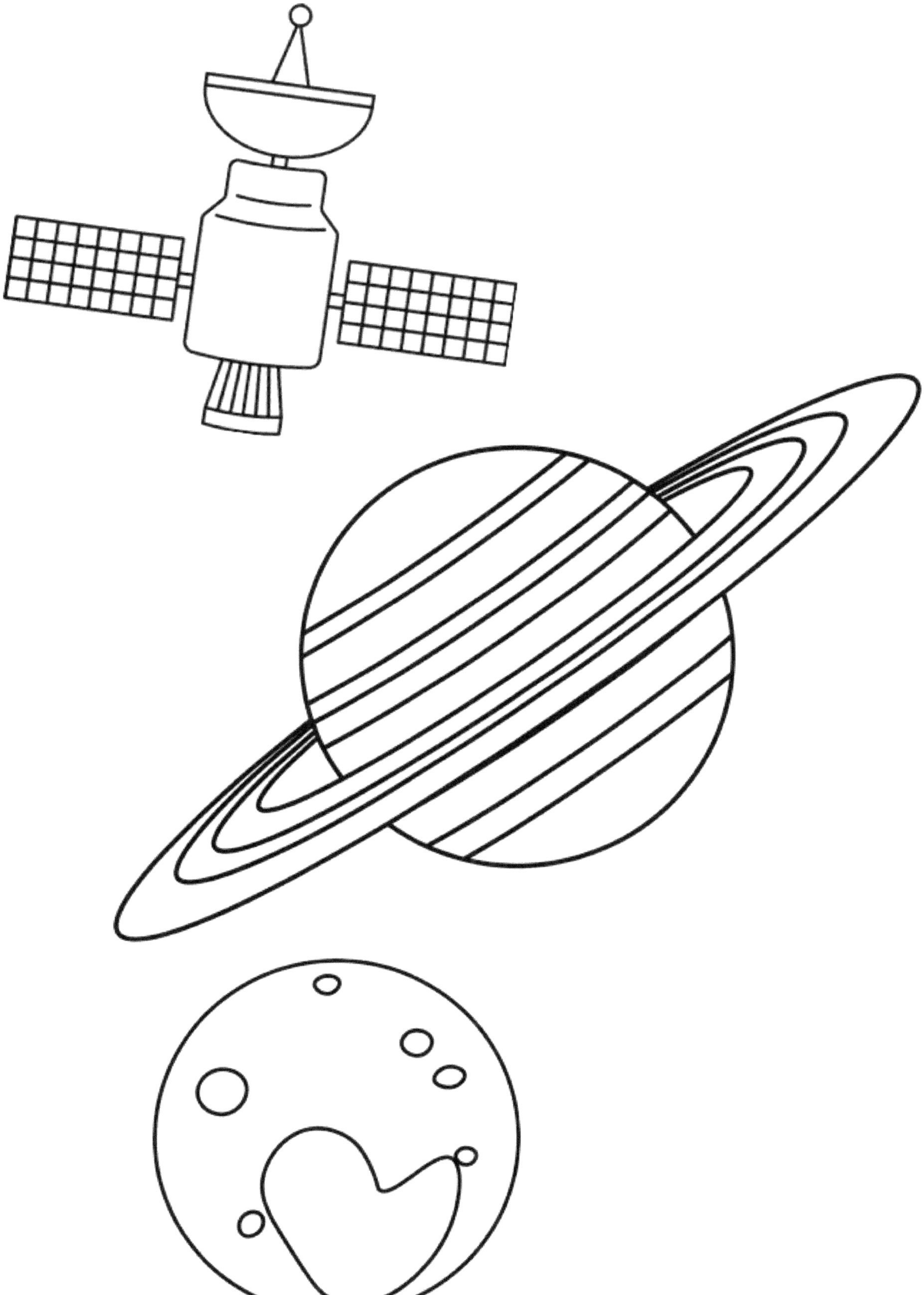

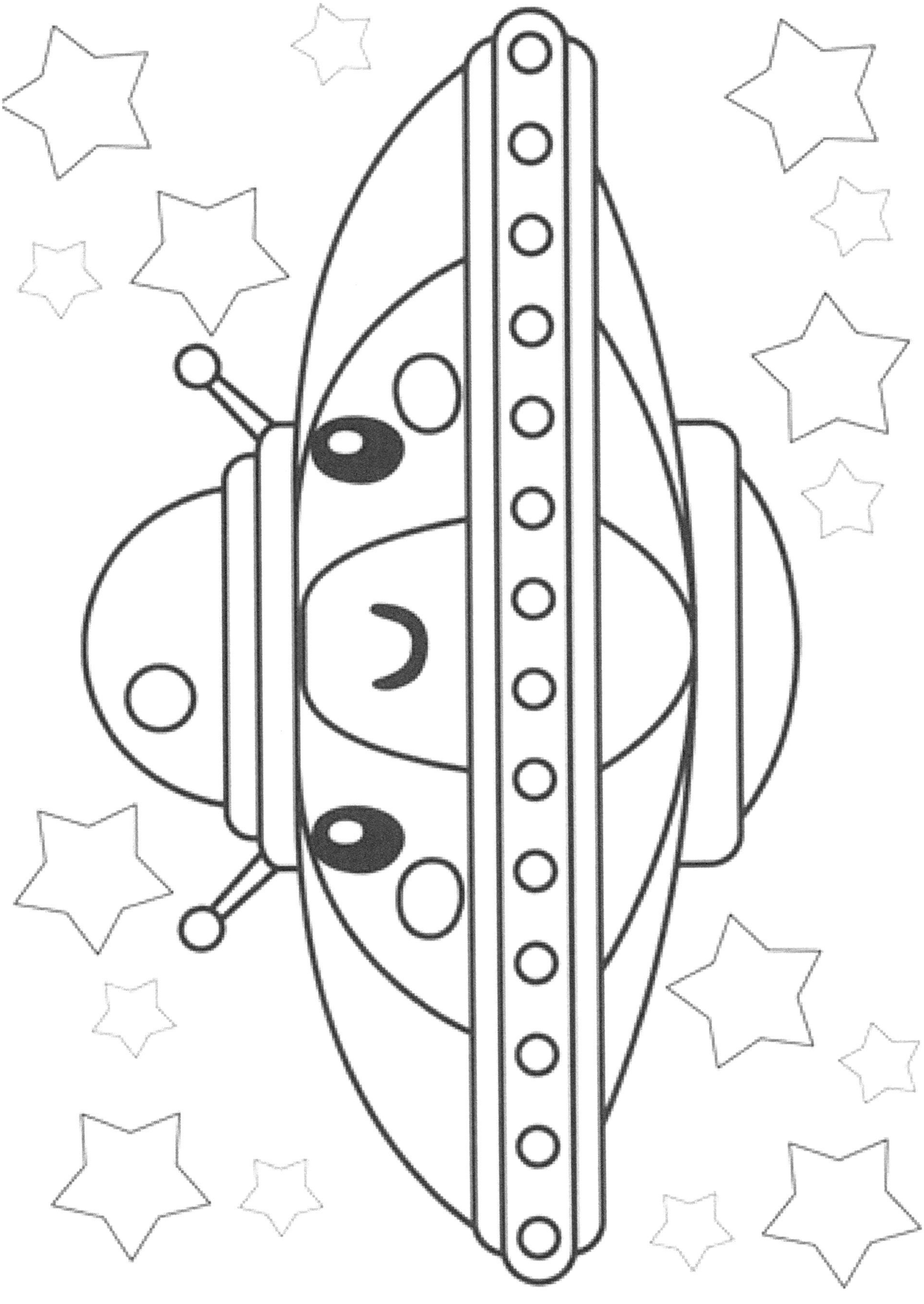

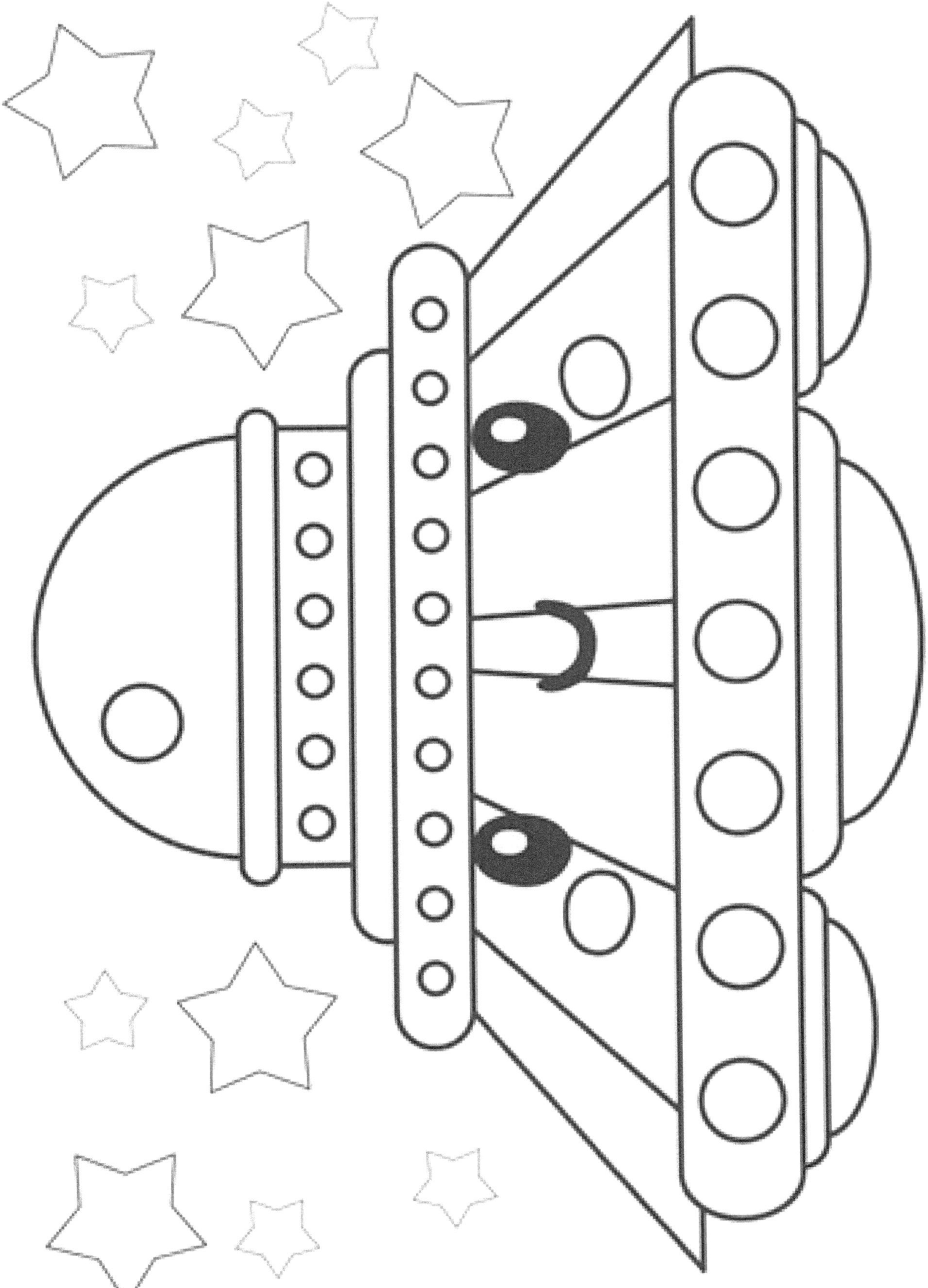

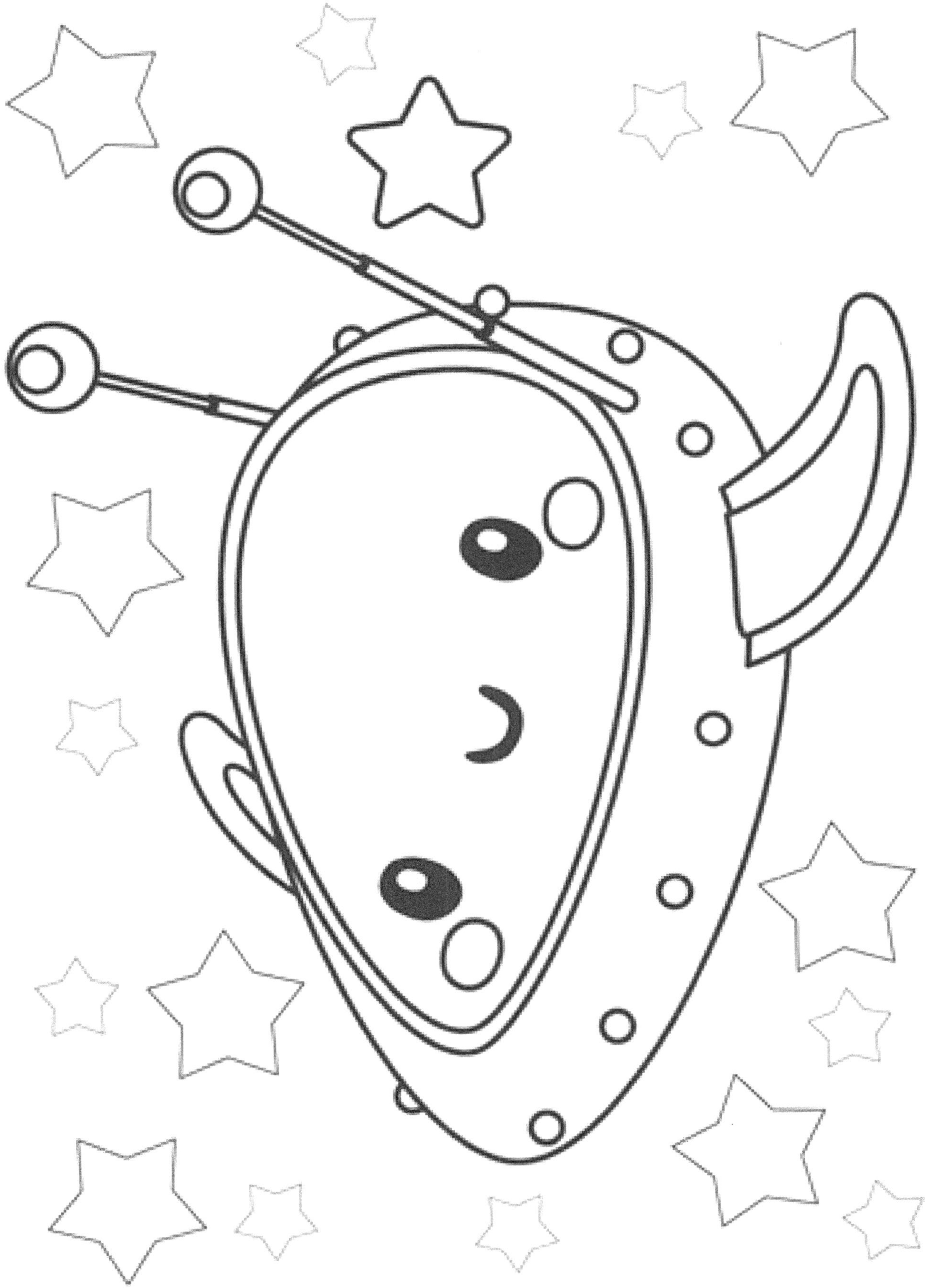

Jupiter

Neptune

Uranus

Sun

Venus

Moon

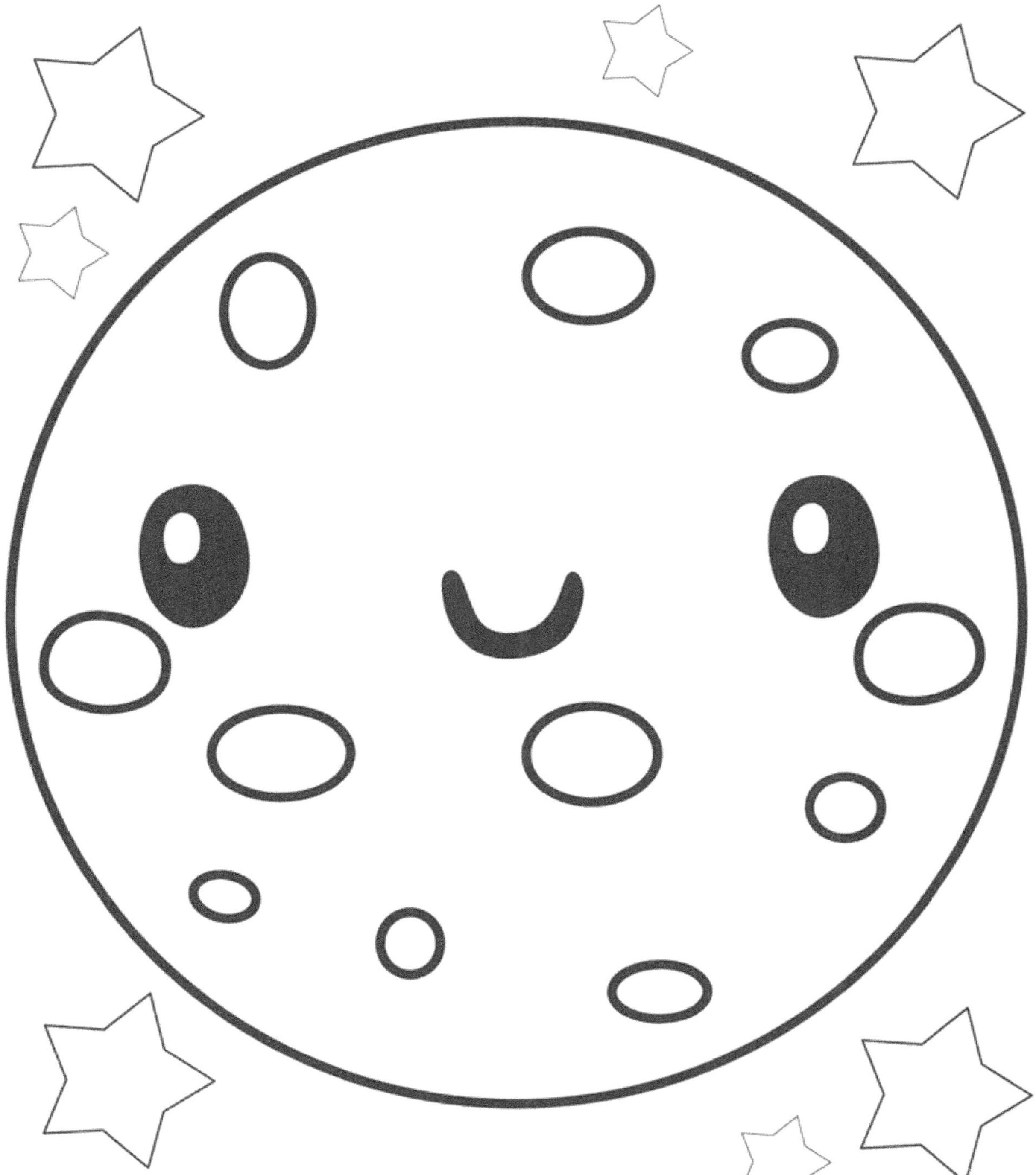

Mercury

Saturn

Pluto

Mars

Earth

Thank you!
I hope your little one enjoyed my solar system coloring book.
Please leave a review.

www.ingramcontent.com/pod-product-compliance
Lightning Source LLC
Chambersburg PA
CBHW062148060526
44654CB00050B/1577
9785303679955